MEDIA SOURCES

TELEVISION

Published by Creative Education
P.O. Box 227
Mankato, Minnesota 56002
Creative Education is an imprint of The Creative Company.

DESIGN AND PRODUCTION BY **ZENO DESIGN**

PHOTOGRAPHS BY Getty Images (David S. Allee, George Diebold,
Richard Freeda/Contributor, Fox Photos, Hummer, Lambert/Archive
Photos, Richard Levine, Hiroyuki Matsumoto, Frédéric Neema,
Petrified Collection, Louie Psihoyos, H. Armstrong Roberts/Stringer,
Walter Sanders//Time Life Pictures, Justin Sullivan/Staff, Gandee
Vasan, Nick Veasy)

LIBRARY OF CONGRESS CATALOGING-IN-PUBLICATION DATA

Bodden, Valerie.
Television / by Valerie Bodden.
p. cm. — (Media sources)
Includes index.
ISBN 978-1-58341-559-7
1. Television—Juvenile literature. I. Title. II. Series.

TK6640.B63 2008
621.388—dc22   2006101004

First edition

9 8 7 6 5 4 3 2 1

MEDIA SOURCES

Television

VALERIE BODDEN

CREATIVE ⓒ EDUCATION

Television (or "TV" for short) is a big part of our lives. You might have watched TV this morning. Or maybe you will watch a TV show tonight.

[5]

MANY PEOPLE WATCH TV IN THE EVENING

The first TV was built almost 100 years ago. But it did not work well. The pictures on the TV screen were not clear.

[6]

At first, some TV stations showed programs only three afternoons a week. Today, you can watch TV every day at any time!

THIS IS AN EARLY TV FROM THE 1920s

Inventors worked to make TVs better. They made the pictures clearer and less fuzzy. Then more people bought TVs for their homes.

PEOPLE USED TO HAVE TO TURN A DIAL ON THE TV TO CHANGE THE CHANNEL. NOW PEOPLE USE REMOTE CONTROLS!

[9]

TVs ARE MADE WITH CLEAR GLASS SCREENS

At first, TVs could show only black-and-white pictures. Then, inventors began to make TVs that could show color pictures. Today, almost all new TVs show color pictures.

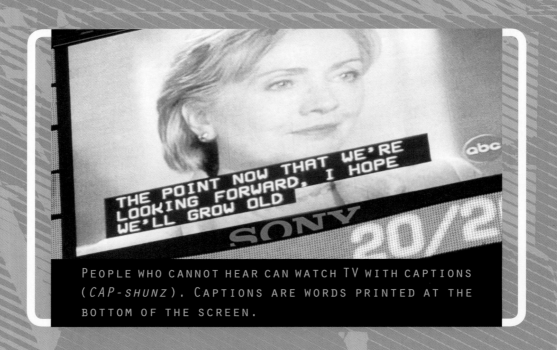

PEOPLE WHO CANNOT HEAR CAN WATCH TV WITH CAPTIONS (*CAP-SHUNZ*). CAPTIONS ARE WORDS PRINTED AT THE BOTTOM OF THE SCREEN.

[11]

MANY NEW TVs HAVE WIDE SCREENS

When you turn on a TV, you see pictures and hear sounds. But those pictures and sounds do not start out inside the TV. They first come from a TV station. The TV station could be in your city. Or it could be far away!

THERE USED TO BE ONLY A FEW TV CHANNELS. TODAY, THERE ARE HUNDREDS OF CHANNELS!

[13]

THIS WOMAN WORKS IN A TV STATION

TV stations use video cameras to **film** TV shows. The cameras turn the shows into TV **signals**. Then the signals are sent out to TVs. Some signals are sent through the air to **antennas** (*an-TEN-uhz*) on homes. Other signals are sent through wires called cables. This is called cable TV.

TV SHOWS ARE FILMED WITH BIG CAMERAS

[15]

[16]

Each TV station has its own channel on TV. Some channels show news all the time. Others show movies. Some show cartoons. Some show all kinds of TV programs.

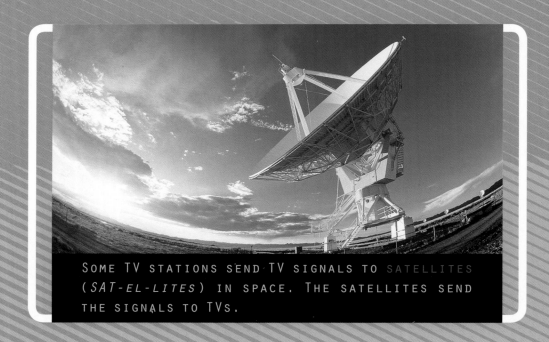

SOME TV STATIONS SEND TV SIGNALS TO SATELLITES (*SAT-EL-LITES*) IN SPACE. THE SATELLITES SEND THE SIGNALS TO TVs.

SOME TV CHANNELS SHOW JUST CARTOONS

When a TV show you like is on, you can watch it right away. Or, you can tape it using a different machine. Then you can watch it any time you want!

ALL PICTURES ON A TV SCREEN ARE MADE UP OF TINY DOTS OF RED, BLUE, AND GREEN.

[19]

PHILIPS MAGNAVOX

TiVo

Now Playing

PHILIPS PERSONAL TV RECEIVER

SPECIAL MACHINES CAN TAPE TV SHOWS

[20]

Today, stores around the world sell all kinds of TVs. Some TVs are huge. Some have flat screens. They can be hung on a wall like a picture! Other TVs are tiny. You can set them on your lap! Inventors keep working to make new, better TVs!

TODAY, MOST HOMES IN THE UNITED STATES HAVE A TV. MANY HOUSES HAVE MORE THAN ONE TV!

[21]

MANY NEW TVs ARE THIN AND LIGHT

GLOSSARY

antennas metal poles that are used to receive TV signals sent through the air

film to make a copy of a TV show using a video camera

inventors people who make new things that have never been made before

satellites big metal objects (some look like boxes with wings) in space that move in a path around Earth

signals pieces of information that tell a TV what pictures and sounds to make

INDEX

4]